Continental Drift

Nancy Gaffield

Continental Drift

Shearsman Books

First published in the United Kingdom in 2014 by
Shearsman Books
50 Westons Hill Drive
Emersons Green
BRISTOL
BS16 7DF

Shearsman Books Ltd Registered Office
30–31 St. James Place, Mangotsfield, Bristol BS16 9JB
(this address not for correspondence)

www.shearsman.com

ISBN 978-1-84861-329-4

Acknowledgements may be found on page 85.

Contents

For Maurice

*"Past
is past. I salute that various field."*
—James Schuyler, 'Salute'

"The notion of a landscape element escapes precise definition. On the one hand, a site may be a physical entity that reveals certain characteristics of the place... On the other, a site may refer to something imperceptible but nonetheless significant (a past event, a local story, or chronology)."
—Christophe Girot

Proem

If only it were possible to arrive
at a condition of knowing
through language. What the rain
knows. That the same number
of planets circle the sun today
as yesterday. That it signals
something. Not exactly Gene Kelly
dancing and singing, but a portent
borrowed from the sea endlessly
rocking and powered by a rage
to meet in time, word to word,
running rings. The surface may appear
fragmented but underneath
a deep and seamless structure. Abides.
This is not about you anymore
but you are in it.

1

Crossing the water

Music of the Phenomenal World

"I have discovered that it is enough when a single note is beautifully played."
—*Arvo Pärt*

ARBOS

The years wind back
to an old refrain

—There isn't a train I wouldn't take
No matter where it's going

A memory of you
fossilised in amber,
out of time.

Looking
for moss under stones
stumbling
upon you.

Disillusions disappear
trailing sound.

I carry you encased
in resin, an amulet
round my neck.

Time trails.

Sound of keys
jangling means a corn bunting
camouflages in the hedgerows.

Feathered choristers utter
the creed
          aural symphony of plain
          song, few notes, much repetition.

Swell
of a single bell.
                    Here before
hear after a tone train streaming
meaning
          unlimited returns.

Swift flight
          of a winter sparrow.

zu Babel

Bittern in the reed beds neck the sky and go boom.
Babbling, inhabiting the borders. That place unreason
lives. Coppiced chestnuts, conifer plantations woods
older than Babylon. European oaks tell of eruption—
yellow fog, dim sun, summer frost, famine. Learning
to weapon, maraud. Bronze follows copper follows
bluebell, anemone, dog's mercury, herb paris, columbine,
bird's nest orchid. Mystery flowers, hordes of swords,
spearheads, sickles, chisels.

Released from dendrochronology pentatonic monody
for four voices. Drones. Rare lady orchid fringes the
escarpment outside time.

*

Loosening the bands of syntax
morpheme by morpheme
mother plaiting pain
the name she gave you
all that remains.

A beam of light
wedges a foot in the door
              elongating

              fa   *fah*   *far*

hum and haw,
random acts of kindness.

You go deep to reassemble
thought.

reccheo, reccho, exile
errant, wretch

Words aged in the dark
before us
stammer past future
present.
Time layers.

Find the word for it
and let it
go into the forest,
locate others.
Tuning.

Among them you walk
in moonlight
carrying your shadow.

*

In the boreal forest
memory frays.

Blur of lore,
dream-work and grasping,
finding your name there. Linked
from the start, your life
and mine.

De Profundis

What matters is

not the frame but the space

inside. Broken glass. The wind

bellows, curtain billows.

Crows there.

A woman stands in front

of the hearth, drying her hair.

All around her the old world

is crumbling. Swathes of red

dead trees. Must not see, say, so

lost without you. Falling masonry. Fire

glances round the room, licking.

Aspen-glow, tinder-box, wild.

West, we were here.

Vor Langen Jahren

The rings of the tree know
something. Radical
introspection. In here is a world
the tree wishes to speak of,
the shadow of a former
Listen.

Overcome by beauty
of wind in the leaves you are
apt to miss the point.
A year is made of light and dark
rings, principle of Limiting Factors. Spring
wood filled with inner light endarkens
and hardens by summer. They died
of heart sickness.
And so a woman
rich in cognates contemplates
the heavens:

str,
étoile, aster, stella, star

Above me sways the fir tree. You are
here not forever
forever not here.
Are you.

★

Berthed in straw
below deck, hemmed in

and the sea roiling. Farewell
to small land and heather village.
Fading. Ruptures,
transatlantic abrasions.
Crossings and starting over.

Scattering
to cheap and fertile
undesired land. Unfamiliar tongue weeds
wed wedes.
                Give me your
Pour through numbered,
encumbered
                No stopping here.

Stumble into pale light,
Lake of the Woods,
someone else's,
dwellers amongst the leaves.
Taking it.
The fields too,
the cistern. Dipping.
Thick as trees and just as good
at keeping secrets.
            Worm in the wood.
Up here on the rim
transubstantiating and wearing
masks, writing the world.

*

Fleeting fall turns to winter sleet.
When they got to the new world
they called each place by the old names.

Never mastered the broad vowels,
learned instead to keep quiet,
tame their speech.

Watching northern geese
baste cloud to earth,
wing dips
pulse in every point,
long and low
herronk of no return.

The heart
repines.

Suppose I were to find
words in my pocket,
loose change. Unlettered.

Blow them over the sea.

What is this spindrift?
asks the cormorant.
Dance of the Spirits
answer the Cree.

*

The bark knows.
Putting on a brave face, it scrutinises
the sky. Day after day, cloud
hangs there. Leaves come and go,
then snow. So much time
spent waiting.

Wave after wave
of lapwings fly
over late-winter fields. Lilacs
in the dooryard
bloom and everything shooting
upwards. A blue orb fractures,
unfamiliar tongue
cleaving, wanting
to sing a song
in a strange land.

Oaks turn
inward.

> *Click-clack*
> *Click-clack*

Shiny refrain of train on the tracks.
Dashing of little ones against stones.
Heart, my heart,
bury my heart.

Adam Laments

Anthracite waves and growing larger.
The sea cambers.

Who goes there?

Tableaux of ravage continuing
past port
past ship
past hope and tearing
train from the track,
sphere slips from its axis.

Little bird too blue to fly
cannot say
what it saw, the sea
took it all.

The palm is the width of,
a foot is the width of,
a pace is four cubits.

The length of a man
        is outspread.

Harmony of symmetry
        is yielding.

Nature of the universe
        spreadeagle.

Language of the body
     in sound
     in place.

They fled for the hills,
bleeding.

Composing themselves
the moon and the nimbus.

                         *

                 —They that carried us away
                     required of us a song

The sun dips
yet its beams linger
on the tree tops to the east.
     If I were bark
     It I were canopy
     I'd shelter you.

The tracks of the deer
winnow through trees
where the whippoorwill calls
and I cannot.

                 —And now down I must sit
         by a little fire, and a few boughs behind me.

They were
     where they not
          effaced.

STABAT

       Mater. Where everything begins,
ends. Black is the water
that covers the earth sweeping,
pulling them deep into the vortex
foundering
and no breathing.

Matter
light as air ascending.
Is there a place for them?

There weep
in deep sorrow
for those who go down
into the sea.

      Mater
have mercy, you who can
stand iniquities. Matter
in these depths
descending

                       mon munde min muna

remember.

2

Inclusions

Sea in Winter

Although the tide fills the space
between a bank of cloud
and a band of shingle,
the sea belongs to the land
today. Shoals of fish spin
in a shaft of silver
light; for a moment
I too am held
in that light.

How little we know
what lies beneath the skin.

My eyes ride the waves.
The sea is self-sufficient.
Across this expanse
the land of my mother,
her people. They have
nothing more
to lose. I am travelling
faster toward them,
gaining velocity
in the wind
blowing down
from the north.

There is too much
sea. We will awake
one morning
no longer knowing
what we are,
why we are here.

The words, when they go,
will leave their shadows
on the steps.

Offshore

Among the waves
a single seagull stays out late
sweeping the sea.
Small beacons flash intermittently.
I wonder if they really exist.

Later I begin to understand
those flashing lights
are the amber eyes of my ancestors
no longer a part
of the material world.
Some words remain with them,
splinters of driftwood, pieces
of sea glass. They invite me to join them
in the clavicle of the sea
where there is just enough
light to make out the features
I have inherited.

When it grows dark footsteps approach
then pass. The stars grimace
though we know tradition demands
a wish. Out there they watch
our comings and goings.
Their silence makes me
uneasy. When night well and truly
falls the only person here
is my shadow dreaming
of a threshold
and wanting to come in.

Flow

I look into the mirror till one of us
blinks, alert to the currents of air and waiting
for the state of flow. I've always wanted
the river to carry me like that. In deep
water the body learns to breathe differently.
Or Millais' Ophelia, her clothes spread wide
awhile. Breaking off communication sweetens
the tongue. Without the complication of syntax
words meet by chance, a reliable guide
I heard a Fly buzz—when I died—

You walked up those tracks to someplace else,
a grand, solitary woman picking up tools
the men left behind. In the gaps between
a world appeared, blending lexicon and landscape.
A state of tension is not compulsory.
Rebel vowels sway to the tune
of a waltz, leaping to an undiscovered place
of reverence and revolt, pulling text
from the dark side of noon
The Stillness in the Room

An aftermath of earlier soundings—
walking through the lives of others,
an interior corridor where a ray of sun
touches the mirror and rainbows ricochet
like bullets round the room. The circumstances
of your birth spun you from your crib. There
were unpredictable sequences, spontaneous changes.
Trauma was part of the landscape.
You didn't get as far as you'd hoped. That prayer
Was like the Stillness in the Air—

Sea-borne, violent, outside the weather cannot
be stanched. The sky grows dark then darker.
The farmer abandons his hay, the seagulls
the plough's churned loam. Lost
for words. It is time to expose the myth;
under the waxy sheen stirs the worm.
What is missing empowers the here
and now. I must retrace your steps,
return to the place where histories form
Between the Heaves of Storm—

Inclosures

Most of us have this same piece of ground
we keep scratching on. Typically one square
metre (or less) marked out sometimes
as one of several for studying the rarest
species. The best shape is the rectangle.
Long short ratio of 25:1. The life histories
of individuals passing through—Pioneer,
Building, Mature, De-generate
phases of growth. They too
have memory, their history determined
by the substrate. Plant them on smooth bare
rock, they will be lichens, on a ribbed surface,
tree moss. And it takes generations
to learn. To compel
memory. To yield.

Winterbourne Valley

1

The valley's thick with fleece
mist and mellow. Crows congregate
picking at things. Propositions
wouldn't melt on their tongues.
It's hard to tell if the horizon's black
shapes are listing ships
or shadows. Broken
spectres. Overnight
giant death's chair mushrooms,
fairy rings veil gill and spore.
So cold in the hour
before dawn, breath clouds.
If you imagine robin egg blue
the sky doesn't fight
them. You lie in a state
of hypnagogia, trying to
step into a name. An astonishment
with all its accessories embedded
folds. Here is a secret
hinterland.

2

In my picture window
seagulls soar, up-lit by late afternoon
sun, newly planted
winter. If I could be
a river running out to sea
I'd start over instead
of sitting
in the same chair
watching the day

wane. Having done so much
that I regret and still
can't let it go. One keeps
sawing away at the knot
in the wood, a dormant bud
around which the fibres flow
in cross sections of vowel
and consonant. Just as a small craft
approaches a waterfall, I ply
an ocean between us
and disaster. Sky of blue
mislaid and later sidewise
a burst of rain roars,
flailing. Like the thin edge
of the wedge, a foot
inside the door.

3
Chill as October lengthened,
a shredded vapour trail
silvered by twilight. I learn
to speak my father's language
with a foreign accent. Some
words are like eggs, they just fit
in the palm of the hand. Others,
webs shimmering with hoarfrost.
I try them all,
roll them round on the tongue,
breathe in their must.
Once I ate a whole
paragraph a sentence at a time.
After that I began to hide some
under the bed. They whisper
to me at night. Wanting me
wanting to burst out.

4

The fog encroaches like a migraine
creeping inward and stealing the visual field.
Your eyes reflect the room's light
and emptiness, an aperture to the exterior
world where the cloud curdles and the sun
turns inward. The sky is
falling, says Chicken Licken. Idleness
bathes the land
in blue milk and suddenly overcome
with relief that the trees
are webbed with wood smoke
you have nothing
to say. Though your body is here

                    it's as if
                you have vanished.

5

Obscure melancholia returns
with November. Leaves resemble
Felina whirling in a West Texas town.
The twist starts here in the calf and travels
to the hip, to the brain. Jagged
veins of lightning thread the sky.
You stagger out from behind
the service station door just as the rain
begins.
                    This is the way
it ends. Tunnel of ivy,
you at the other end. I am not
on line, not in the room. I've simply stepped
out of it on a grey and gloomy day.
To ask what is this? For
high in the fleeting clouds the hawks

draw figure eights, riding
the thermals to rise higher
or just for the sheer hell of it.

Solid objects

We are in quagmire. No one can find
the malaise, but it's in there,
alright. Burrowing in the joists,
reconfigured. In our fifties we
were alone, but by the time we reached sixty
there were so many of us. Here I reach for a trope,
but all I find are some tokens scattered
around. Like the image of the candlestick that is also
two faces. Objects, persons, places.
The background matters, that it's in there, absorbing.
Sedges and shrubs, mosses and lichens,
crowberries growing on a treeless mountain
tract. Mapless space. The lost
family of water leaving
the ground soggy. Only a faint glow
of light visible at mid-day and pursued
by blue twilight. Who will remember
the names when we are gone?

'Things the mind already knows'

A storm cloud, darker
denser more volatile
oozes over the hill
and dissolves into a plume
of smoke with a passion
for flocking. White
Flag. The surface signifies
nothing. Stars built up
from the surrounding merest
suggestion. Bits of newsprint and fabric
dipped in beeswax. An open field
of stripes over-painted with white
oil and blotted out. Forty-eight
revenants who want to remain
anonymous. Spectral
secrets hidden in the gunk
hinting. Complicated
lives, drifters outside
looking in. Like white
washing the fence
it has to be hard to get
to want it. Wide roads and open spaces,
squares connecting what isn't.
Complacency sitting in an easy chair.

Mappa mundi

A response to Robert Frank's 'The Americans'

Your external world is my T and O map.
A circled landmass cut with a T
and me at the top keeping a difficult balance.
Like those photographs of the real Americans
riding along on the crest of a wave, US 285
through New Mexico, silver ribbon
heading straight to infinity
or hell. No people but when you do see them
they're always looking away. Together
but solitary. Land lots of and the starry
sky creating a third voice. Fade
to cityscape: Hoboken NJ in three parts,
two windows divided. Brick walls make
good neighbours inside each
staring out. The flag hoisted by its own,
bigger than anything. Bigger than America
but devoid. Now look below the window,
at the street, the glass, a bus going by.
You can see them standing at the rear,
occluded. If we could only get back to 1959,
get our bearings. But everything has a schedule
and you are not what you think ontologically.

Landscaping the High Plains

Now the prairie life begins—
thick brakes of alder give way
to purple sage and wide spreading plains.
You follow three chords
and the truth,
the twang
of the high lonesome.

Cicadas ratchet it up
a notch confusing the wind
vortices. Encounters
with the workings of Manifest Destiny
are far from casual.

Odd things happen
when you get out of town

      Hardly a driver
          Is now alive
              Who passed
                  On hills
                      At 75

Don't I know it

To tend water, you need to know the contingencies
of weather, stay tuned
to the wind. Directional forces are cyclical.

Take the rain swollen by late spring
run-off in full flow. Sandy,
turbulent. The rain falls and it is not

the same world. Later on
at the beach we had a debate
about the raisin pudding theory.

The nucleus is surrounded by an orbit
of electrons, you said, it is a question
of physics. No, it is a desecration

of planets. Where were you in October
1962? I don't want to sound complaining
but you know there's always rain

in my heart. I'm the only person
who knows where
I slept that night. Escaped

MAD that time. You don't need to tell me
how close we are to the edge.

Dust

it begins in the house
of bad moods
it begins again
as a mote
as memory

it begins as
a stable structure in the rain
rainbows   of oil
          certain themes
are incurable

who are you   in your prospect
of puddles

nothing stays in its proper place
unsettled landscape   nuclear
sublime
          if you don't
want to know
look away   now

3

PO-WA-HA

And if he stopped short?

she crosses   the Arkansas
the trail scattered with sand hills

not a blade
        of grass

                     false-ponds
           deceive

Farewell   my own   countree

Well inside   fine water
          sprinkling the dirt floor
          to keep down   dust

               Amongst
     the "white-faced Warriors"
          a woman gave birth
                         and after
          half an hour
she went   to the river
                         and   breaking ice
          bathed herself

The Navajo came among them then
        and carried off some twenty

Quiver-full of arrows   dressed in
striped blanket   a string of beads

Oxen turned out
        wagon   upset
        and all the bales on the ground

Pity him and pass on

                                Not married
            no more

Buffalo   horse   and gun
overlanders   overhunted
        overgrazed
                landscaped
        the High Plains

        exhausted   the water
        fired
                the grasslands

cattle carried tuberculosis
        buffalo cut down

I have come here to stand
      in a grove of cottonwoods   surrounded
      by bluffs   they reproach
      me for being remiss

The passing of every old woman
      or old man   means
the passing of some tradition

Wide ladder of granite
      ruined walls of yellow sandstone
wind sings in the cliffs   yearning

Silver spruce and aspen pull me
      towards grey exile

a long way North of dangerous

teriors of commonplaceness
indelible memory of place [moving on]

Desert of the Anasazi
Desert of the whirlwind dancing across mesas
Desert of quivering air
Desert of the glittering world surrounded by six mountains
        Sierra-Oscuro-shadowed desert—peripheral,
                incandescent desert

      "For every atom belonging to me as good
      belongs to you."

Houses, bodies, plants—everything is a temporary abode
through which po-wa-ha flows.

Pity and pass on, for Gadget's in the garden.

Dressed in a seersucker suit
Mister Gadget   is brooding

Geopolitical pushing and shoving
            new form of energy   accident
                  of geography

Constant rain   drips
            from the eaves
            from the faucet   blotting out
all sound but itself
            and his thoughts

                  shift to the wooden shrines
            and temples of Kyoto   sentimental
            and highly combustible
top of his list   of targets

He convenes a meeting   condemning
            the tender souls
            who advocate a demonstration

No one raises any objection

People do not count

                    Other echoes
inhabit the sands

                              Don't forget me

The dark-eyed La Tules
perches on her human footstool

        at the junction of Palace Ave & San Francisco St

The Santa Fe trail brings in
travellers   townsfolk   wayward youth
          mano a mano
these boys learned the mysteries
of Monte   by losing

The scalp is the principal
part of the business

                        Nooned it
on the bank of the Cimarron
            seeing is   /   seeing as
I pick up a buffalo skull
            some brown wool
            still attached

                        Soon a thunderstorm
rejoices me

Inside
            inside myself
                        there is a world

Desertum: an abandoned place
red land   ore
colourless selenite crystals cool
            to the touch   once
covered by a shallow sea

steep, crescent-shaped dunes
constantly in motion

                                        peripateo

"the verb calls it
        into being"

Gadget was delivered by a Plymouth sedan

                              final assembly
                        a dust-proof bedroom
                     in the Valley of the Shadow
                  Camino Real / Sierra Oscura

                        amongst mountain lions
                              bighorn sheep
                        the succulent yucca

The men advance
        long-trousered & long-sleeved
        (never wear black)
        they apply sun cream
        sunglasses & welders' goggles

The radio played *Serenade for Strings*
        O prayed to an atomic god
        to break
              [b]low
                    burn and
                          [m]ake new

A sustained roar knocked them down
        the flash so bright they could see
        the bones through their hands

A searing light of beauty and clarity
  "the poets dream about but describe most poorly"
   says Mister Gadget
  "success beyond imagination"

                    peripateo

Alamogordo

        clarity of light
        late evening

watermelon glow   gunmetal grey veil of distant rain

        the Rio Grande rift, geologically young and dynamic

            "There is a God and an intelligent purpose
        back of everything"

Convergence of histories
Gadget changes everything
implosion test
hoisted to the belfries

        letting it go
        creating the first cataclysm
        mushroom cloud site
            catechism recite
                (goggled watchers stand back)

sand thereabouts turns to glass   earth trembles

Later no one sniffing the trace of air
can say
        who you were   only
the thud of the   stopped
            clock

Someone with big hands
    speaks across the ages
        No quarter asked or given

Here at the Heart of the World
    the earth shakes

sheet lightning scrambles
    the upper clouds   distant storm

Spider Grandmother stoops low
    gathers in her hands
    some sand   letting it
        run out in a thin stream

    spinning it into a whirlpool   she
        steps in

"the flames do now rage and glow"

"Germany will make a most interesting subject for the
initial experiment. Japan can be used to provide a
confirmation."

If you unite a number of small fires
            and in the case of a congested
            residential area
drop thousands of cylinders of thermite
            you create perfect conditions
            for setting alight
            a city of paper

You may begin to comprehend

                                    what is lost
                        in moonlight and a wind
                                    from the north

A firestorm more fearsome than ever witnessed
            against which
            every human
            resistance

                        A strange howling
of a tornado
of flame

juttering in the updraughts   the silver tails of the planes
            just visible in clouds of black smoke
                                    like the embers over a campfire
                        "put together of many bright shining splinters"

nothing between them
           and hell   but the air

Some said it was a dream
        come true   properly kindled
        Japanese cities   burning
                   like autumn leaves

           (Mister Gadget
      is getting ready

The boys on the hill were finding their way
      through labyrinths of linkage

Piston-driven locomotion
     cavorting with   historical residue

disturbance   drive to know
     swerving   and falling
     off the edge   going back
          to connect the dots

     you are   therefore   I am

the conditions of occurrence
     charged   interactions
     with / against

mokusatsu

Don't forget

Pine River   blocked
        by water   river's natural barrier
        no exit

Mufu Mountain   too many
        to bury   too many
        to burn
                bodies dumped in the River
        sea of blood   then

"worse mutilated than any I ever saw"

                                        pikankan

        Beneath the shield of Purple Mountain
cold sleep of winter   time stands still

        We are   incidental
                to strategic purpose
        We are   not born
                to live   or even
                to survive

The sun appeared again this morning
        I don't know how   it dares
                to show its face

At the mouth of the river
watery lanes of red lotus blossom
and dismembered parts
float
out to sea

mokusatsu

the road to Dead Man's Lake hard
          and level

rapid shifts from irreparable frags

the kindly breeze   aloft

immaculate   radiation
          tensile light

                                        pikadon

my whole life

has hung far too long
          upon a lie   flying off
          in bright flecks

Those cities   still busy with disposing
       continued   to count
       among the corpses

they found   an aluminium lunch box
       the lunch still inside
       the shadow   only
       the shadow   of a human body

Those cities   astonished by an energy they couldn't
                             grasp
       the complete bands of radiation
       travelling at the speed of light

eraiyo
cried the mothers

Those cities   peopled by a ghost parade

osoroshii
cried the children
petechaie   the sign of worse to come

"I think it's good propaganda. The thing is these people got good and burned—good thermal burns."

"That's the feeling I have," said Mister Gadget.

The wood warbler spins
a coin on a marble slab
slipping in some soft, sad notes

Accident of geography
    Spider Grandmother
stands in the doorway   overlooks
    the fallen
       masonry
    the borders
      blur
    flute-edged arrowheads   artefacts

      linguistic sediment   further layering

we are
    all of us
      born of them

peripateo

you walk the boundaries
      marking territory   they (mis)took

you cannot
      wipe the slate clean
            language gets used
      over and over again
            re-coupling

letting see
      what has been hidden
            underneath

"How that red rain doth make the harvest grow"

Stepping into the old river   alone
          in this strange world
the strangeness of red dirt

                              water
                                        wind
                                                  breath

recrossing the old trails   still here

you are in the desert
          and it is in you

carrying a corvid feather   iridescent
          black luck

its light   the void
          where everything
begins

the initial lines   are guidelines
          the web
          beginning from the outside
          in
          replacing one
          spiral with another

Spider Grandmother is waiting
          on the edge

you walk on
                    the dead

4

The Lay
of the Land

Unconsolidated debris

O   tireless oarsman   you
                    who open the ways
          know
the northern gate of the sky

I was in a dream
                    and in that dream
          a few polished bones
                    and boots   at the edge   of
                    the moraine
caught up
          in the web of his [s] tory

I was in a dream   and in that dream
          I saw   a land   destroyed
                    by water

I wrote you letters
                    bent your ear
                    to maintain
the dialogue

The diggers   when they came
          discovered the perforation
                    the door
          intact

(we had swept away   even   our footprints)

Those diggers   discovered   the death mask
          inlaid with precious
                    lapis and malachite
they carried it   away

In my dream   it is summer
       I am reading your letter
              in the garden
     It says:

You are here   you
should start
    where you are

Voler

traverser of waves
            swathes
of geese fall from the sky
        whiffling
                    so
            lost

        terrified
                of winter   they
        steal away
                south   we

        min them

                        every landscape
is a palimpsest

                        they afforested
everywhere
        they felt like it

                            repairing breaches
                            to keep things
                        from disappearing

    clean wounds
        close quickly
                in upland air

Disharmonic folds

Distant borrowing takes in
    the mountains
    the foothills
        the pathos of things

across the valley floor   a cold wind blows
    the place is seismic

a rotation may not be enough to reach a different
    condition   it may be necessary
    to add an imaginary translation

it's easy to lose one's way   in the forest
    blue deer   move between
    firs
        pining

they know how to live
    with   out
leave things alone

above the timberline   a sudden snowstorm
    blurs the valley below
there is never a complete return

a possibility   to say
    the only thing you ever wanted
    was to live   amongst

Adjacent borrowing

sentences flow in a single direction
        plucking stones   new fractures
        leave the landscape jagged

human interference builds distinct soil
        horizons   heaped
        though hidden

bedrock plays a role
        in the lay of the land
        see *esp.* the Dentelles

Jurassic lace   Montmirail
        folded and forced into
        admirable spikes

the longer things stay
        the more rubble
        gets dumped

when the train pulls out
        at last   passing towns
        with no names

you breathe in   breathe
        out   leaving
        behind   left

Grey zone

An occluded front currently lies across southwest Britain
bringing patchy rain. An area of low pressure and an associated
frontal system will move east and bring rain across southern areas
throughout the day. Continued cold with a brisk southeasterly
wind. Unseasonably cold for April.
                              The day is

                                              ashen
                                              dingy
                                              dove
                                              drab
                                              dun
                                              graphite
                                              grizzled
                                              gun-metal
                                              leaden
                                              pewter
                                              plumbago
                                              mole
                                              slate
                                              steel
                                              stone

paradeigma trying (a)verse
            the day begins
                    in silence   you silent as a clam lately
I look where you are not
            it makes you   all the more   present

on the Eastern Sea Road   the boundary
            between is weak

                                          upward borrowing
clouds deflect   overhead
            a helicopter scrambles the seagulls

it's getting late

PAC-3 missiles in strategic locations

whatever happens   relations   drift
          or

what does it mean   when

[Es]cape

Landscape of childhood, Midwestern farmland and deciduous forest with excursions into the High Plains. Wooden houses, weathered red, low-lit, long-shadowed. A broad brown river and learning to read. The landscape as a complex language nested within a sentence, landschaft, landschap, landskip, languescape. An old house hoards its memories.

Something happens when you dislodge the outward aspect of the familiar. A border has been crossed. You become a world-builder. Place-making means multiple acts of remembering. *Pas à pas* imagination slides between the frames of reference. Not opposition, but apposition. We go by side roads.

It's time to return borrowed things. Distant borrowing of heather village, the Lake of the Woods, the High Plains and those cities of paper. Adjacent Borrowing, Winterbourne Valley, the woods and the fields, the stillness in the room. Upward borrowing, the sound of the farewell bell. Lapwing and crow, plumbago sky. Downward borrowing of mosses and lichens, fallen masonry. *Mono-no-aware*: the pathos of things.

When the work is done it is time to go.

Notes to the Poems

Music of the Phenomenal World
This cycle of poems was inspired by listening to Arvo Pärt's *Arbos*.

"There isn't a train I wouldn't take..."
From 'Travel' in *Second April* (1921), Edna St. Vincent Millay.

"They that carried us away required of us a song" —Psalm 137:3.

"And now down I must sit by a little fire, and a few boughs behind me"
in *A Narrative of the Captivity and Restoration of Mrs.
Mary Rowlandson.*

"I heard a fly buzz—when I died—"
Emily Dickinson, '465' in *The Complete Poems*.

The poem 'Inclosures' uses quotation from Charles Olson's poem
'Maximus to Gloucester, Letter 27 [withheld].'

"Things the mind already knows"
Jasper Johns, speaking about his painting of 1955, 'White Flag'.

MAD: mutually-assured destruction.

po-wa-ha
wind/water/breath; the creative life force of Pueblo cosmology.

And if he stopped short?
"The politician being interviewed clearly takes a great deal of trouble to
imagine an ending to his sentence: and if he stopped short? His entire
policy would be jeopardized."
Roland Barthes, *The Pleasure of the Text*.

the "white-faced Warriors"
Term used to refer to the American Army, Susan Magoffin's *Down the
Santa Fe Trail and into Mexico*.

Jornada del Muerto
The day's journey of the dead man in the Jornado del Muerto desert

basin, an 80-mile stretch of desert with no water in New Mexico; site of the Trinity bomb test.

"For every atom belonging to me as good belongs to you."
    Walt Whitman, *Song of Myself.*

Gadget —The code name given to the first bomb tested.

"the verb calls it into being"
    William Carlos Williams, 'The Desert Music.'

"break, blowe, burn and make new"
    John Donne, 'Holy Sonnet 14' as quoted by Oppenheimer on the occasion of the Trinity Bomb Test.

"the poets dream about but describe most poorly… success beyond imagination"
The words uttered by Brigadier General Leslie Groves, who was in charge of the Manhattan Project. He selected the target cities; he wanted to bomb Kyoto but was over-ruled.

"There is a God and an intelligent purpose back of everything."
Church Deacon and physicist Arthur Holly Compton, involved in the Manhattan Project.

"the flames do now range and glow"
    Jonathan Edwards, 'Sinners in the Hands of an Angry God',
    (Sermon).

"Germany will make a most interesting subject for the initial experiment. Japan can be used to provide a confirmation."
    Air Marshall Sir Arthur Harris. The firestorms in Tokyo on
    March 9–10, 1945, reportedly killed 100,000 people.

"put together of many bright shining splinters"
I.I. Rabi said of J. Robert Oppenheimer: "Oppenheimer was a man who was put together of many bright shining splinters."

mokusatsu
Translated from Japanese as, "Take no notice; treat the matter with silent contempt."

"worse mutilated than any I ever saw"
Testimony of Mr John S. Smith, 1865, on the Sand Creek Massacre by U.S. Army Colonel John Chivington and his troops.

pikankan
Translated from Japanese as, "Let's see a woman open up her legs." This comes from the testimony of a former Japanese soldier who spoke about the rape and murder of Chinese women in Nanking for the documentary *In the Name of the Emperor* (Chang 49).

pikadon
Translated from Japanese as " flash/boom."

eraiyo
Translated from Japanese as "It is too heavy."

osoroshii
Translated from Japanese as "It is too much to bear."

"I think it's good propaganda... That's the feeling I have."
Memorandum of telephone conversation between General Groves and Lt. Col. Rea at Oak Ridge Hospital, 9 a.m. 25 August, 1945.

"How that red rain doth make the harvest grow"
Lord Byron, 'Childe Harold's Pilgrimage,' Canto III.

Distant borrowing/adjacent borrowing
"shakkei", or borrowed scenery, is a concept in Japanese landscape gardening with four categories: distant borrowing (of mountains and lakes), adjacent borrowing (of neighbouring features), upward borrowing (of clouds, stars, weather), downward borrowing (of pounds, rocks, leaves, earth).

Mono-no-aware
Translated from Japanese as "the pathos of things."

Bibliography

Barthes, Roland. *The Pleasure of the Text*. Trans. Richard Miller. New York, NY: Hill & Wang, 1980.

Chang, Iris. *The Rape of Nanking*. New York, NY: Penguin Books, 1997.

Dickinson, Emily. *The Complete Poems*. Ed. Thomas H. Johnson. London: Faber & Faber, 1975.

Drumm, Stella, ed. *Down the Santa Fe Trail and into Mexico: The Diary of Susan Shelby Magoffin, 1846-1847*. Lincoln, NE: The University of Nebraska Press, 1982.

Edwards, Jonathan. "Sinners in the Hands of an Angry God Sermon," Enfield, CT, July 8, 1741. October, 2012. www.ccel.org/ccel/edwards/sermons.sinners.html

Frank, Robert. *The Americans*. Washington, DC: Steidl National Gallery.

Girot, Christophe. 'Four Trace Concepts in Landscape Architecture.' *Recovering Landscape: Essays in Landscape Theory*. Ed. James Corner. Princeton, NJ: Princeton Architectural Press, 2000. 59-68.

Gordon, George (Lord Byron). *Lord Byron: The Major Works*. Ed. Jerome McGann. London: Oxford Paperbacks, 2008.

Grouett, Stephane. *Manhattan Project: The Untold Story of the Making of the Atomic Bomb*. Lincoln, NE: An Author's Build Backinprint. com Edition, 1967, 2000.

Lewis, Jon, ed. *The Mammoth Book of Native Americans*. London: Constable & Robinson, 2004.

Olson, Charles. *Selected Poems of Charles Olson*. Ed. Robert Creeley. London: University of California Press, 1997.

Rosenthal, Nan. 'Jasper Johns (born 1930).' In *Heilbrunn Timeline of Art History*. New York: The Metropolitan Museum of Art, 2000. September, 2012. www.metmuseum.org/toah/hd/john/hd_jo hn.htm

Rowlandson, Mary. *The Narrative of the Captivity and the Restoration of Mrs. Mary Rowlandson* (1682). September, 2012. http://www. library.csi.cuny/edu/dept/history/lavendar/rownarr.html

Schuyler, James. *Collected Poems*. New York, NY: Farrar, Straus and Giroux, 1993.

Selden, Kyoko and Mark, eds. *The Atomic Bomb: Voices from Hiroshima and Nagasaki*. Armonk, NY: Eastgate Book, 1989.

St. Vincent Millay, Edna. *Collected Poems*. New York, NY: Harper and Row, 1956.

Weigle, Marta, ed. *Telling New Mexico: A New History*. Santa Fe, NM:
Museum of New Mexico Press, 2007.

Whitman, Walt. *The Complete Poems*. London: Penguin Classics, 1996.

Williams, William Carlos. *The Collected Poems Volume II 1939-1962*.
Ed. Christopher MacGowan. Manchester: Carcanet Press, 2000.

Acknowledgements

I am grateful to the editors and publishers in which the following poems in this book originally appeared, often in somewhat different forms:

Section 4 of the poem 'Winterbourne Valley' appeared in a Templar (2011) pamphlet entitled *Owhere* as 'Undone Business'. The poem 'Solid Objects' appeared as 'The Years'. The poems 'Mappa Mundi' and 'Things the mind already knows' also appeared in *Owhere* (Templar 2012).

The poems 'De Profundis', 'Vor Langen Jahren' and 'Dust' appeared in *Molly Bloom, the Third* [online]. www.mollybloompoetry.weebly.com

The poem 'Flow' appeared in *Poetry Review*, Summer 103:2.

The poems 'Adjacent Borrowing' and 'Voler' appeared in *Zone* magazine.

The poems 'De Profundis', 'Vor Langen Jahren' and 'Dust' appeared in *Molly Bloom, the Third* [online magazine] mollybloompoetry.weebly.com

I wish to thank The Poetry Trust for the generous gift of a week's protected writing time on the Suffolk Coast, where some of the poems in this collection were written.

Thanks also to Howard Bowman, Patricia Debney, Emmi Itäranta, Nancy Fulton, Janet Montefiore and Jeremy Scott.

Special thanks to David Herd.